To

_____

on the occasion
of the
christening of

_____

on

_____

Other giftbooks by Helen Exley:

Baby Record Book   Welcome to the New Baby
To a very special Daughter   To a very special Son

Published simultaneously in 1997 by Exley Publications in Great Britain, and
Exley Giftbooks in the USA.
Copyright © Helen Exley 1997
The moral right of the author has been asserted.

Quotations selected by Helen Exley.
Paintings and borders by Shirley Trevena, R.I. (living artist)
All the borders and motifs are details taken from the paintings that
appear in this book.

Printed in China.

12 11 10 9 8 7 6

ISBN: 1-85015-926-2

Acknowledgements: The publishers are grateful for permission to reproduce copyright
material. Whilst every effort has been made to trace copyright holders, the publishers
would be pleased to hear from any not here acknowledged. RACHEL CARSON: Extracts
from *A Sense of Wonder* by Rachel Carson, copyright © 1956 by Rachel L. Carson, renewed
1984 by Roger Christie. Published by HarperCollins Publishers. CHRISTIAN PUBLICITY
ORGANISATION: Prayer reprinted with permission of CPO - Design and Print. MARIAN
WRIGHT EDELMAN: Extracts from *Guide My Feet* by Marian Wright Edelman. © 1995 by
Marian Wright Edelman. Reprinted by permission of Beacon Press, Boston and Russell &
Volkening as agents for the author. Extract from The Order of Service for the
Thanksgiving for the Birth of a Child from THE ALTERNATIVE SERVICE BOOK 1980,
copyright © The Central Board of Finance of The Church of England and is reproduced
by permission.

Exley Publications Ltd, 16 Chalk Hill, Watford, Herts WD19 4BG, UK.
Exley Publications LLC, 232 Madison Avenue, Suite 1409, NY 10016, USA.
www.helenexleygiftbooks.com

A
CHRISTENING
GIFT

A HELEN EXLEY GIFTBOOK
PAINTINGS BY SHIRLEY TREVENA

EXLEY
NEW YORK • WATFORD, UK

*A*ll of us are gathered here
on your christening, to wish you well
as you start your life's journey.
You are so small and look so vulnerable,
it's hard to think that soon you will be
setting out on life's path with all its pitfalls.
And yet, all of us here today, pledge
to help you along that path, offering our
support as you take the courage to make
your own choices, and find your own
way in the world.

A PARENT'S PLEDGE

I promise to...
Listen to my children and communicate
   with my children
Teach my children right from wrong
   Be a good role model for my children
Spend time with and pay attention to
   my children
Educate my children in mind, body,
   and soul

Work to provide a stable family life
   for my children
Pray for and see God in my children
   and in all children
Vote for my children to ensure them
   fair opportunity
Speak out for my and other people's
children's needs.

MARIAN WRIGHT EDELMAN,
FROM "GUIDE MY FEET"

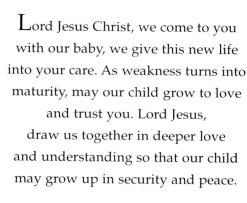

Lord Jesus Christ, we come to you
with our baby, we give this new life
into your care. As weakness turns into
maturity, may our child grow to love
and trust you. Lord Jesus,
draw us together in deeper love
and understanding so that our child
may grow up in security and peace.

CHRISTIAN
PUBLICITY
ORGANIZATION

TO THE CHILD

This is your special day, although you will not remember it or even know what it means. Yet, we want you to know that we are all here for you, not just for today, but every day that we possibly can for the rest of your life.

LISA SCULLY-O'GRADY

If one could give a child a Godmother's gifts – then surely they would be perception, courage, love – and hope.

CHARLOTTE GRAY

Parents, relatives and friends gathered here today,
have so many wishes for you. Too many to list.
Noble wishes for honesty, kindness and wisdom.
Material wishes for wealth, health and good looks.
Well some wishes come true and some don't.
However much we want to, we can't protect you
from all life's hurts. One day you'll understand
why. So, more than all our wishes and hopes,
there's one thing we can promise you: that we
will always be here to support and help you, in
good times and in bad.

CARL FREEMAN

DEAR CHILD...

I *wish you the gift of empathy –*
  the ability to stand in another's shoes
  and know their needs.
I wish you kindness – given as a gift
  and not as an obligation.
I wish you perception – to see
  without bigotry or self-esteem.
I wish you courage in all the hard times
  you will meet – a heart and mind
  that learns from failure – and finds hope even
  at the edges of despair.

I wish you praise for work well done,
    the satisfaction of achievement,
    the joy of creation.
I wish that you become a person that shines
    with kindness and intelligence
    and love of life.
I wish you an exploratory mind
    and respect for the beliefs of others.
I wish you the love that changes
    and grows with every year
    that passes.

PAM BROWN,
b.1928.

Mankind
OWES TO CHILDREN
THE BEST IT HAS
TO GIVE.

UNITED
NATIONS
DECLARATION

A BABY COSTS MORE
THAN ANYTHING ELSE
ON EARTH.
YOUR LOVE, YOUR LIFE.

PAM BROWN,
b . 1 9 2 8

Babies

*B*abies are bits of stardust
blown from the hand of God.

LARRY BARRETTO

A newborn baby ... is without question
the most phenomenal, the most
astonishing, the most absolutely
unparalleled thing that has yet occurred
in the entire history of this planet.

IRVIN S. COBB

Babies are such a nice way
to start people.

DON HEROLD

Every baby born into the world
is a finer one than the last.

CHARLES DICKENS
(1812-1870)

A baby is God's opinion
that the world should go on.

CARL SANDBURG
(1878-1967)

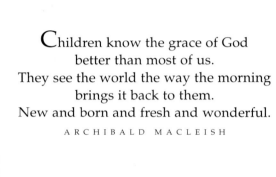

Children know the grace of God
better than most of us.
They see the world the way the morning
brings it back to them.
New and born and fresh and wonderful.

ARCHIBALD MACLEISH

Always smile back at babies.
You could be the one to destroy their
conviction that all the world loves them.

PAM BROWN,
b.1928

There is still a child in all of us who has always believed in miracles.
To children miracles are simple things.
Every day is miraculous – unexplained, inspiring, ever new.

KAREN GOLDMAN

Babies are living jewels,
dropped unstained from heaven.

SIR FREDERICK POLLOCK

The baby has learned to smile,
and her smiles burst forth like
holiday sparklers, lighting our hearts.
Joy fills the room.
At what are we smiling?
We don't know, and we don't care.
We are communicating with one another
in happiness, and the smiles are
the outward display of our delight
and our love.

JOAN LOWERY NIXON

When children are,
there is the golden age.

NOVALIS
(1772-1801)

When the voices of children
are heard on the green
And laughing is heard on the hill,
My heart is at rest within my breast
And everything else is still.

WILLIAM BLAKE
(1757-1827),
FROM "NURSE'S SONG"

"I have many flowers," he said,
"but the children are the most beautiful
flowers of all."

OSCAR WILDE (1854-1900)

Blessed be childhood,
which brings down something of heaven
into the midst of our
rough earthliness.

HENRI FREDERIC AMIEL

*Once the children were in the house
the air became more vivid and more heated;
every object in the house grew more alive.*

MARY GORDON

*What feeling is so nice as a child's hand
in yours? So small, so soft and warm,
like a kitten huddling in the shelter
of your clasp.*

MARJORIE HOLMES

*One laugh of a child
will make the holiest day more
sacred still.*

R.G. INGERSOLL

*Child, you bringest to my heart the babble
of the wind and the water, the flowers'
speechless secrets, the clouds' dreams,
the mute gaze of wonder of
the morning sky.*

RABINDRANATH TAGORE
(1861-1941)

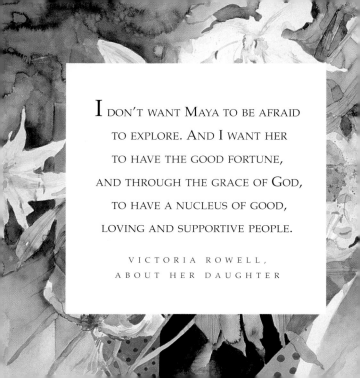

I don't want Maya to be afraid
to explore. And I want her
to have the good fortune,
and through the grace of God,
to have a nucleus of good,
loving and supportive people.

VICTORIA ROWELL,
ABOUT HER DAUGHTER

IN EVERY WORK THE BEGINNING
IS THE MOST IMPORTANT PART,
ESPECIALLY IN DEALING WITH ANYTHING
YOUNG AND TENDER.

SOCRATES

To show a child what has once delighted
you, to find the child's delight added to your
own, so that there is now a double delight
seen in the glow of trust and affection,
this is happiness.

J.B. PRIESTLEY
(1894-1984)

What children are looking for is a hug,
a lap, a kind word, a touch, someone
to read them a story, somebody to smile
and share with.

JOHN THOMPSON

A child's hand in yours –
what tenderness and power it arouses.
You are instantly the very touchstone
of wisdom and strength.

MARJORIE HOLMES

If you want your children to turn out well,
spend twice as much time with them and
half as much money.

H. JACKSON-BROWN, JR.

There's no such thing as a kid who needs
fixing.... They're born with everything.
And what most people do is squash it
and take it away from them.

ROBERT BLAKE

We should seize every opportunity
to give encouragement.
Encouragement is oxygen to the soul.

GEORGE M. ADAMS

Never fear spoiling children by making them too happy. Happiness is the atmosphere in which all good affections grow – the wholesome warmth necessary to make the heart-blood circulate healthily and freely.

ANN ELIZA BRAY
(1790-1883)

If you want to teach your children well, be a model of kindness and compassion. Let the example you set be one of understanding and generosity.

AUTHOR UNKNOWN,
FROM RANDOM ACTS OF KINDNESS

My dream for Ashley and Alexandra is to raise them to be all they can be, to nurture them into responsible, loving, secure, giving, human beings who not only find, but aren't afraid to go after, whatever it is that makes them happy in life.

VANESSA BELL CALLOWAY

Judge your success as a parent to the degree that your children feel safe, wanted, and loved.

H. JACKSON-BROWN, JR.

The value of children

*I*f there were no other reasons
(though we know there are as many
as stars), this alone would be the value
of children: the way they remind you
of the comfort of simplicity.
Their compelling common sense.
Their accessibility and their honesty.
Their lack of pretense.

ELIZABETH BERG

God sent children for another purpose
than merely to keep up the race –
to enlarge our hearts; and to make us
unselfish and full of kindly sympathies
and affections; to give our souls
higher aims; to call out all our faculties
to extended enterprise and exertion;
and to bring round our firesides
bright faces, happy smiles, and loving,
tender hearts.

MARY HOWITT
(1799-1888)

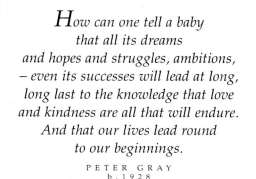

*H*ow can one tell a baby
that all its dreams
and hopes and struggles, ambitions,
– even its successes will lead at long,
long last to the knowledge that love
and kindness are all that will endure.
And that our lives lead round
to our beginnings.

PETER GRAY
b . 1 9 2 8

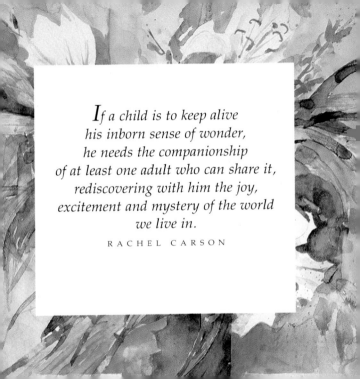

If a child is to keep alive
his inborn sense of wonder,
he needs the companionship
of at least one adult who can share it,
rediscovering with him the joy,
excitement and mystery of the world
we live in.

RACHEL CARSON

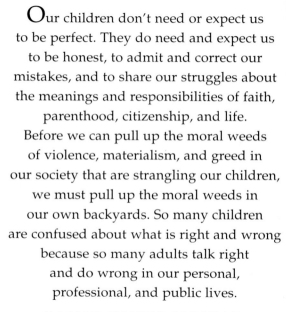

Our children don't need or expect us
to be perfect. They do need and expect us
to be honest, to admit and correct our
mistakes, and to share our struggles about
the meanings and responsibilities of faith,
parenthood, citizenship, and life.
Before we can pull up the moral weeds
of violence, materialism, and greed in
our society that are strangling our children,
we must pull up the moral weeds in
our own backyards. So many children
are confused about what is right and wrong
because so many adults talk right
and do wrong in our personal,
professional, and public lives.

MARIAN WRIGHT EDELMAN,
FROM "GUIDE MY FEET"

THERE IS JUST ONE WAY

TO BRING UP A CHILD

IN THE WAY HE SHOULD GO,

AND THAT IS

TO TRAVEL THAT WAY YOURSELF.

ABRAHAM LINCOLN

(1809-1865)

We can't give our children the future,
strive though we may to make it secure.
But we can give them the present.

KATHLEEN NORRIS
(1880-1966)

The training of children is a profession,
where we must know how to lose time
in order to gain it.

JEAN JACQUES ROUSSEAU
(1712-1778)

Let me look upward into the branches of
the flowering oak and know that it grew great
and strong because it grew slowly and well.

WILFERD A. PETERSON

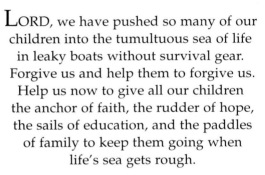

LORD, we have pushed so many of our
children into the tumultuous sea of life
in leaky boats without survival gear.
Forgive us and help them to forgive us.
Help us now to give all our children
the anchor of faith, the rudder of hope,
the sails of education, and the paddles
of family to keep them going when
life's sea gets rough.

MARIAN WRIGHT EDELMAN,
FROM "GUIDE MY FEET"

If we are to teach real peace in this world
and if we are to carry on a real war
against war, we shall have to begin
with children; and if they will grow up
in their natural innocence,
we won't have to struggle, we won't
have to pass fruitless, idle resolutions,
but we shall go from love to love
and peace to peace, until at last
all the corners of the world are covered
with that peace and love for which,
consciously or unconsciously, the whole
world is hungering.

MAHATMA GANDHI
(1869-1948)

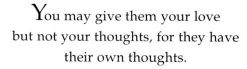

You may give them your love
but not your thoughts, for they have
their own thoughts.
You may house their bodies but not
their souls for their souls dwell in
the house of tomorrow, which you
cannot visit, not even in your dreams.
You may strive to be like them,
but seek not to make them like you.
For life goes not backward nor tarries
with yesterday.

KAHLIL GIBRAN
(1883-1931)

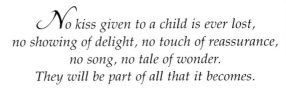

No kiss given to a child is ever lost,
no showing of delight, no touch of reassurance,
no song, no tale of wonder.
They will be part of all that it becomes.

PAM BROWN,
b.1928

In the person whose childhood has known
carresses, there is always a fibre of memory that
can be touched to gentle issues.

GEORGE ELIOT
[MARY ANN EVANS]
(1819-1880)

The first duty to children
is to make them happy.
If you have not made them so,
you have wronged them.
No other good they may get
can make up for that.

BUXTON

Children will not remember you for
the material things you provided
but for the feeling that you
cherished them.

RICHARD L. EVANS

MY DREAM FOR SAVANNAH, KOPPER
AND CHEYENNE IS THAT THEY WILL GROW
INTO BEAUTIFUL YOUNG WOMEN
WHO LOVE THEMSELVES AND THEREFORE
DON'T NEED TO BE VALIDATED
BY ANYONE ELSE....

JAYNE KENNEDY OVERTON,
ABOUT HER DAUGHTERS

CHILDREN ARE LIKELY
TO LIVE UP TO WHAT YOU
BELIEVE OF THEM.

LADY BIRD JOHNSON

Dear God,

I thank You for the gift of this child to raise, this life to share, this mind to help mold, this body to nurture, and this spirit to enrich. Let me never betray this child's trust, dampen this child's hope, or discourage this child's dreams.

MARIAN WRIGHT EDELMAN,
FROM "GUIDE MY FEET"

GOD OUR FATHER,
IN GIVING US *THIS CHILD*
YOU HAVE SHOWN US YOUR LOVE.
HELP US TO BE TRUSTWORTHY PARENTS.
MAKE US PATIENT AND UNDERSTANDING,
THAT *OUR* CHILD MAY ALWAYS
BE SURE OF OUR LOVE AND GROW UP
TO BE HAPPY AND RESPONSIBLE;
THROUGH JESUS CHRIST OUR LORD.
AMEN.

FROM
"THE ALTERNATIVE
SERVICE BOOK"

If a child lives with criticism,
he learns to condemn.
If a child lives with hostility,
he learns to fight.
If a child lives with ridicule,
he learns to be shy.
If a child lives with shame,
he learns to feel guilty.
If a child lives with tolerance,
he learns to be patient.
If a child lives with praise,
he learns to appreciate.

If a child lives with fairness,
he learns justice.
If a child lives with security,
he learns to have faith.
If a child lives with approval,
he learns to live himself.
If a child lives with acceptance
and friendship,
he learns to find love in the world.

FROM
"YOUR BABY'S BAPTISM"

Hush Baby. I will keep you safe.
Though the winds of the world buffet
at the door.
I will keep you safe till you are grown
and strong enough to stand alone.
And even then I will always be here
as comfort, refuge, breathing space,
when you need me, as long as you need me.
With love, a listening ear and a hot dinner.
Always.

PAM BROWN.
b.1928

If I had influence
with the good fairy who
is supposed to preside
over the christening of
all children,
I should ask that her
gift to each child in
the world be a sense of
wonder so indestructible
that it would
last throughout life.

RACHEL CARSON